Polio:
A Frightening Disease

"Wellbee" says
BE WELL!
take
ORAL
POLIO
VACCINE
• tastes good
• works fast
• prevents polio

Written by Bridie Dickson

Flying Start
to Literacy®

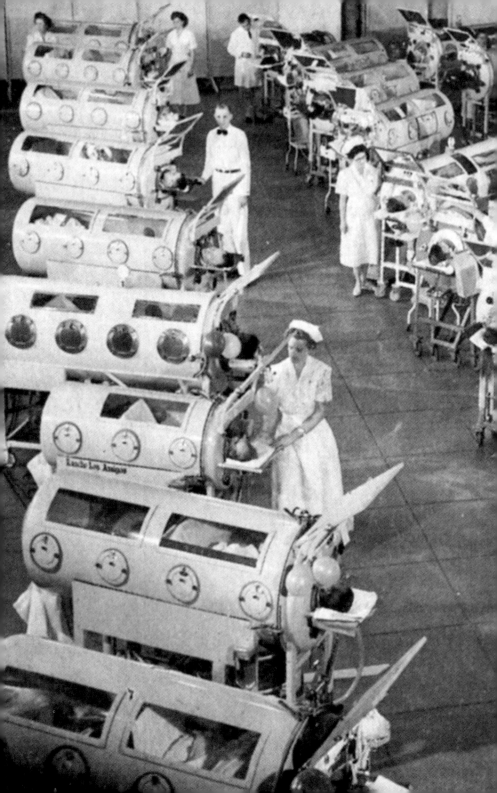

Contents

Helen's story

When six-year-old Helen visited her sick cousin Adrian, no one knew that he had a disease called polio. He later became very sick and was never able to walk again.

After the visit, Helen began to feel unwell. She had a headache, pain in her arms and legs, and a stiff neck. She began to feel worse and could no longer walk without falling over. One of her arms and both her legs were completely paralysed. Helen was rushed to hospital in an ambulance.

Six-year-old Helen

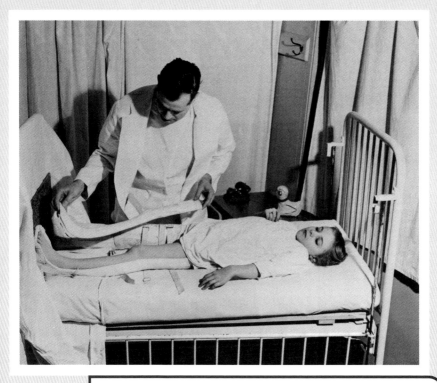

A doctor at the hospital is examining Helen's legs. She had casts on her legs that were easy to remove.

It was the 1940s and children all around the world were getting polio. It was highly contagious.

The family's worst fears were realised when Helen was diagnosed with polio. Helen remained at the hospital, while her family was placed in quarantine. For three weeks, the family was not allowed to leave their home and no one could visit them. None of Helen's family could visit her.

Helen remained in hospital for nine months. She was strapped to a full body splint – a wooden frame – so that she could not move. Along with other polio patients, she was wheeled outside on her hospital bed to get fresh air and sunshine. For short periods, she was released from the splint to be bathed and to receive physical therapy, where her muscles were exercised.

Polio patients were wheeled outside the hospital to watch a children's show.

Polio patients in class with their teacher

After Helen returned home from the hospital, she remained in a splint for much of the time. Eventually, she improved enough to attend school, where she was given treatment for her weakened muscles.

By the time Helen was seven years old, the strength in her legs had improved and she was able to walk with leg braces called calipers. As one of her legs was now longer than the other, she also needed to wear a built-up shoe. Her walking was slow, but it gave Helen a sense of freedom and independence.

Throughout her life, Helen received medical care and worked hard to strengthen her body. She later become a teacher and had a family of her own.

Chapter 1

Why people feared polio

During the first half of the twentieth century, people lived in fear of catching polio. In countries all around the world, including Australia and the United States, children were becoming infected with polio. From the 1930s to the 1950s, tens of thousands of people were infected each year.

What is polio?

Polio is a disease caused by a virus that attacks the nervous system. This is a system of nerves in your body that sends messages to and from your brain to make parts of your body move and feel things.

At first, people infected with the virus get flu-like symptoms. Then, instead of getting better, they can become a lot worse. The symptoms include muscle spasms and pain, loose and floppy limbs, and sudden paralysis. A small percentage of patients die when their lung muscles stop working and they cannot breathe.

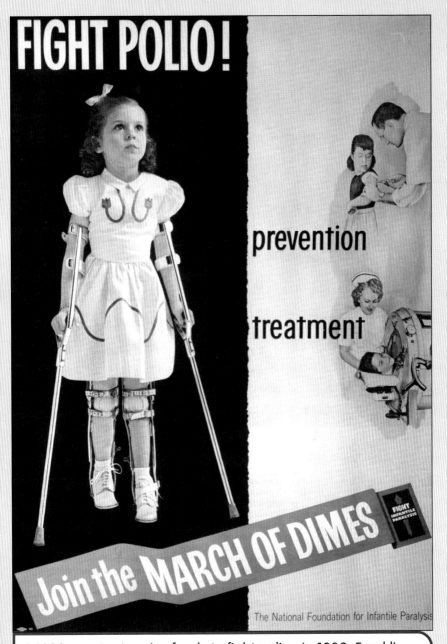

A 1930s poster to raise funds to fight polio. In 1938, Franklin D. Roosevelt, who had polio, was the President of the United States. He set up a fund to raise money to use for research into developing a polio vaccine. The fund became known as the "March of Dimes".

Polio spread rapidly

It is easy to understand why people were terrified of polio. By the 1950s, polio was spreading rapidly throughout towns and cities, creating fear in communities. Healthy children suddenly became very sick, seemingly without warning. Some were paralysed and some died.

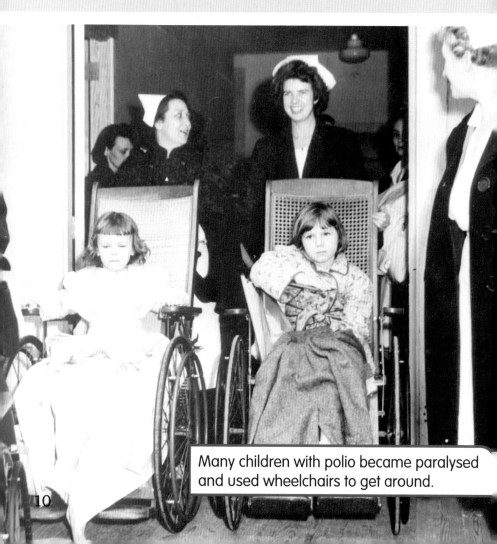

Many children with polio became paralysed and used wheelchairs to get around.

Polio is contagious and spreads through physical contact.

Polio spreads from one person to another through hand-to-hand or physical contact, and young children are most at risk. But, not much was known about polio infection at the time. People knew that polio was a contagious disease, but there was no information on how it was spread or how to stay safe. This lack of knowledge added to people's fear.

The polio epidemic

In 1937, Australia experienced one of the worst polio epidemics ever. During the summer of 1937–38, about 2000 people in Tasmania caught the disease and 81 people died. Victoria was also hit hard during this summer. The disease spread throughout Melbourne and into country areas, with over 2000 reported cases and a staggering 109 deaths. Tragically, most of these cases were children.

Protecting the children

Parents felt helpless. How could they protect their children? Many parents went to great lengths to try to keep their children safe. Some people tried to protect their children by reducing their contact with others. They kept their children away from swimming pools, parties and playgrounds.

A young girl with polio and her father look at a poster that shows her being treated.

Some people went to even greater lengths and sent their children to live in the country where there were fewer people and therefore fewer chances of catching polio.

Communities tried to stop young people from spending time together – swimming pools and movie theatres were shut, sporting competitions were cancelled and sometimes schools were closed.

These children are taking a train to the country because their parents thought they would be safer from polio there.

Chapter 2

How was polio treated?

Like any virus, polio cannot be cured with medicines. Doctors could only treat the symptoms. Some people never fully recovered from polio. They had difficulty walking without aid for the rest of their lives.

Many children who survived polio were left with lasting problems, including pain and muscle weakness. Some polio survivors never regained the use of their muscles and required help to walk. Some learned to walk again using crutches or calipers and some used a wheelchair.

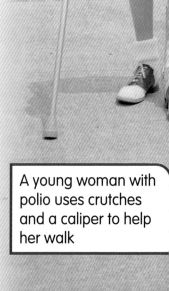

A young woman with polio uses crutches and a caliper to help her walk

14

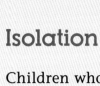

Isolation

Children who contracted polio were separated from the community. They were usually taken to a hospital and placed in isolation, away from other patients. This was to prevent further spread of the disease.

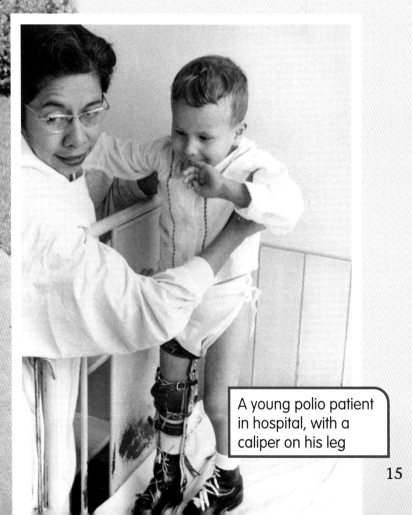

A young polio patient in hospital, with a caliper on his leg

Wooden frames and splints

At the time, the main form of treatment was to keep patients completely still so they couldn't move. Patients were strapped to wooden frames or splints. The idea behind this practice was that it stopped patients' muscles becoming deformed by strong muscle spasms. Many patients were kept in splints for months and even years.

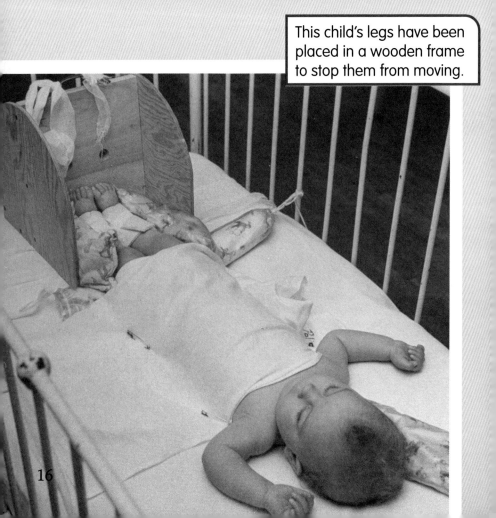

This child's legs have been placed in a wooden frame to stop them from moving.

Iron lungs

Some children with polio needed help just to continue breathing because the muscles in their chests were unable to work properly. These children were put into a machine called an iron lung, which helped them to breathe.

In the 1950s, many hospitals had whole wards filled with patients in iron lungs. Most polio patients were kept in iron lungs until their lung muscles starting working properly again. This often took two to three weeks.

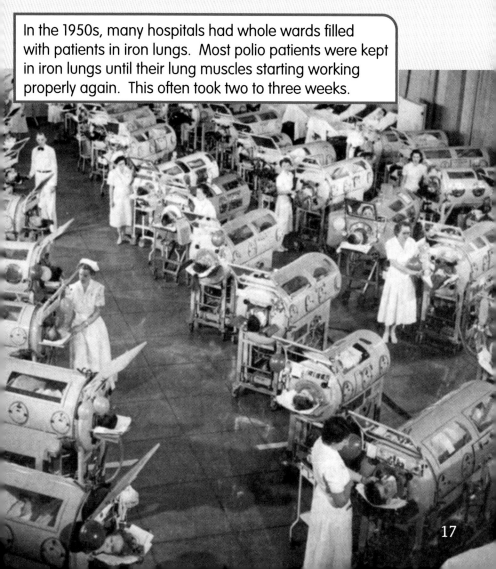

A new approach

Not everyone agreed that using splints and wooden frames was successful. Another approach was to treat the affected limbs with therapies such as massage and movement. As time went on, this approach to treating polio victims was slowly introduced and accepted.

Sister Kenny's new treatment

Sister Kenny was born in Australia in 1880. At the age of 20, with experience as a nurse, she began helping people who were ill, including polio patients. Unaware of the standard use of splints, she suggested that patients apply heat and gently exercise the muscles that had been paralysed. The patients improved and recovered.

Australian nurse, Sister Kenny

In 1932, Sister Kenny set up a clinic to treat long-term polio victims. She treated these patients with hot baths, warm lotions and massage. She got rid of calipers and encouraged her patients to move their limbs. However, when Sister Kenny demonstrated her methods, doctors made fun of her. But this didn't stop her.

Sister Kenny helps a young polio patient to strengthen his leg muscles

In 1940, Sister Kenny decided to travel to the United States to promote her methods. Despite initially having almost total opposition from the medical world, support for Sister Kenny kept growing. Her treatment methods continued to help polio victims and, in 1942, The Sister Kenny Institute was built in Minneapolis, Minnesota. More and more clinics were set up to implement her methods. Sister Kenny trained doctors from around the world to treat polio.

Polio patients exercise their muscles in a swimming pool.

Chapter 3

A medical breakthrough

In the 1940s in Australia, New Zealand and the United States, the number of people affected by polio kept increasing. Scientists and medical researchers urgently searched for a vaccine that would protect people from polio.

In 1947, an American medical researcher called Jonas Salk began work on finding a polio vaccine.

Jonas Salk at work in his laboratory

Testing the vaccine

In 1951, after years of painstaking work, Salk and his team tested the vaccine on children who already had polio, which ensured that the trial would be safe. He measured their levels of antibodies before vaccination and was excited to see that the levels were raised significantly by the vaccine. The trial took three years and was a success.

After the trial, Salk was confident that his vaccine was safe, so he vaccinated himself and his family. His team and their families also had the vaccination.

By 1954, the vaccine was ready to be tested on more than one million healthy children. Everyone was very nervous, especially Jonas Salk. Would the vaccinations be a success or a failure? No child involved in the testing got polio.

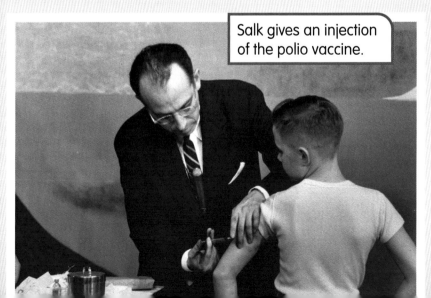

Salk gives an injection of the polio vaccine.

Vaccination begins

A year after the trial began, the results were announced to the world. On 12 April 1955, the vaccine was declared to be "safe, effective and potent". The vaccine had worked!

People were jubilant and celebrations broke out everywhere – schools were closed, factory whistles blew, church bells rang, people cried with relief!

The polio vaccine was rapidly introduced to other parts of the United States and then to the rest of the world. In Australia, the first polio vaccinations took place in 1956. This vaccination changed the world. It saved many, many lives and made people feel safe.

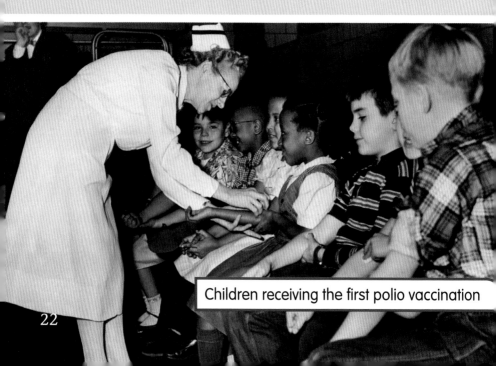

Children receiving the first polio vaccination

Another vaccine

Another American researcher, Albert Sabin, was also working hard to create a polio vaccine. Unlike Salk's vaccine, which was injected directly into the bloodstream, Sabin's vaccine could be taken by mouth.

In 1961, it was approved for manufacture in the United States. Before long, Sabin's vaccine was also being used all around the world, including Australia, where it was introduced in 1966.

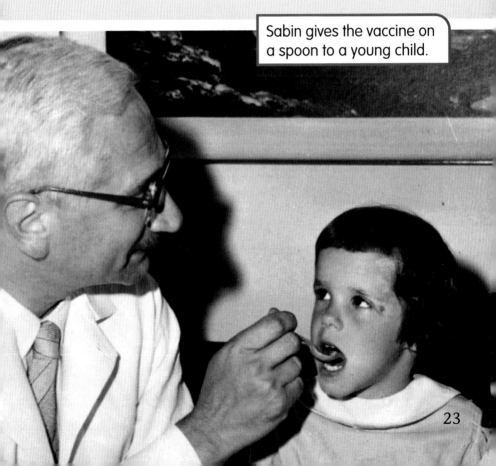

Sabin gives the vaccine on a spoon to a young child.

Toward a polio vaccine

Jonas Salk and Albert Sabin worked tirelessly for years to develop a polio vaccine. Both men were successful and have helped the world become free from polio.

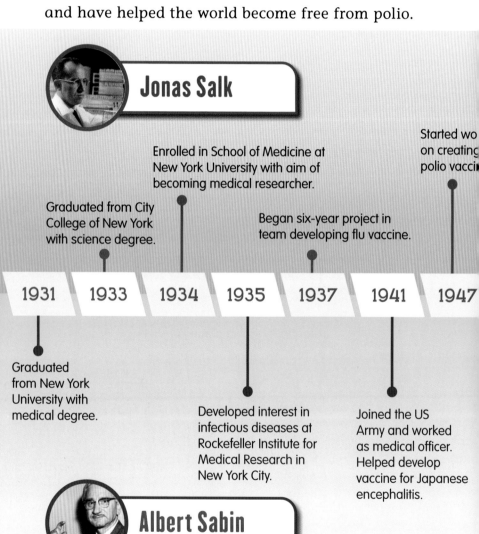

Jonas Salk

Enrolled in School of Medicine at New York University with aim of becoming medical researcher.

Started wo on creating polio vacci

Graduated from City College of New York with science degree.

Began six-year project in team developing flu vaccine.

| 1931 | 1933 | 1934 | 1935 | 1937 | 1941 | 1947 |

Graduated from New York University with medical degree.

Developed interest in infectious diseases at Rockefeller Institute for Medical Research in New York City.

Joined the US Army and worked as medical officer. Helped develop vaccine for Japanese encephalitis.

Albert Sabin

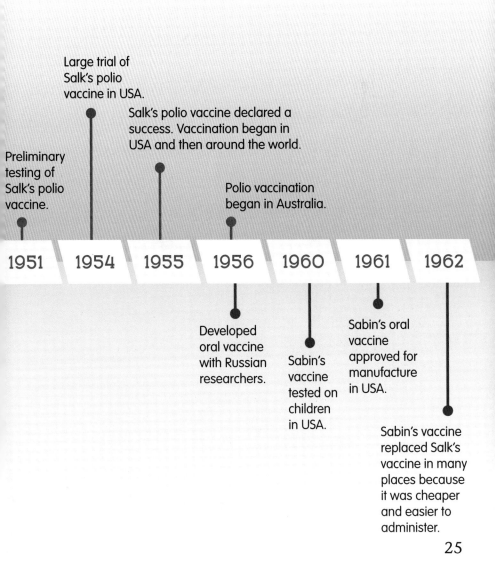

Large trial of Salk's polio vaccine in USA.

Salk's polio vaccine declared a success. Vaccination began in USA and then around the world.

Preliminary testing of Salk's polio vaccine.

Polio vaccination began in Australia.

1951 **1954** **1955** **1956** **1960** **1961** **1962**

Developed oral vaccine with Russian researchers.

Sabin's vaccine tested on children in USA.

Sabin's oral vaccine approved for manufacture in USA.

Sabin's vaccine replaced Salk's vaccine in many places because it was cheaper and easier to administer.

Chapter 4

Hope for a polio-free worl

Today, most people receive the polio vaccine when they are babies. But in some places, not everyone is vaccinated and the threat of polio is still real. People are still catching the polio virus, becoming sick and dying.

To eliminate the threat of polio, health organisations around the world are working towards having every child vaccinated for polio. By doing this, the polio virus will eventually die out. It is hoped that one day the polio virus will be gone forever.

Today, most children are protected against polio, because they receive the polio vaccine when they are babies.

Protection for one, protection for all

Communities of people benefit from being vaccinated. When 80 to 85 per cent of people in a community are vaccinated against polio, it helps to protect the whole community. The chances of a disease such as polio spreading from person to person are greatly reduced. This protects ALL members of the community, even those that have not been immunised. This is called "herd immunity".

Did you know?

Some people cannot be vaccinated against polio. Some are too young and some have an illness that makes their immune system too weak. These people rely on everyone else being immunised to remain safe from polio.

Helping everyone

Why isn't everyone vaccinated for polio? Some people miss being vaccinated because they live in very remote places and it is difficult for them to get to health centres.

Sometimes people are not vaccinated because they live in parts of the world where there is war, conflict or other problems.

The challenge for health organisations is to reach every child in the world and to give them the polio vaccination. The world is very close to totally eliminating polio, but there is still work to do!

A health worker gives the polio vaccine to children living in a remote area.

Eradicating polio

Global efforts to eradicate polio throughout the world began in 1988. The dark areas show polio outbreaks.

1988
350,000 cases of polio

2003
Fewer than 700 cases of polio

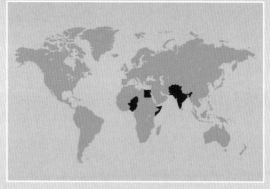

2015
74 cases of polio

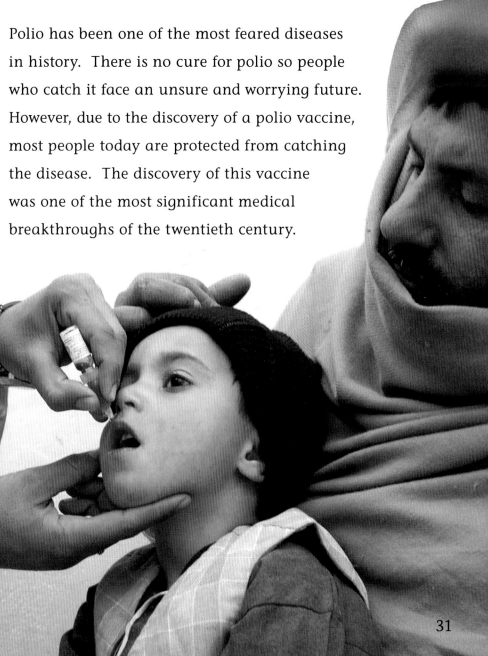

Conclusion

Polio has been one of the most feared diseases in history. There is no cure for polio so people who catch it face an unsure and worrying future. However, due to the discovery of a polio vaccine, most people today are protected from catching the disease. The discovery of this vaccine was one of the most significant medical breakthroughs of the twentieth century.

Glossary

antibodies   substances produced by the body to fight disease

contagious   spread from one person to another through physical contact

immune system   system that protects the body from infections and diseases

paralysed   not being able to move or have any feeling in a part or all of the body

quarantine   a state of being kept away from others to prevent the spread of disease

symptoms   a feeling of illness or change in the body caused by a disease

vaccinate   to give a vaccine to prevent a disease

vaccine   a substance given as an injection or a medicine that you can drink to protect against a particular disease